The First Family of
HOPE

The
OBAMAS

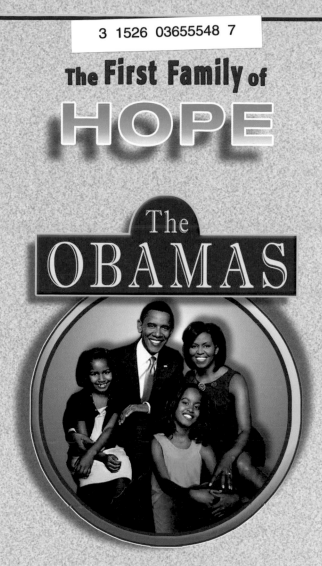

Barack

Michelle

Malia

Sasha

The Obama Family Tree

Obama Mania

The Obama Family Tree

Hal Marcovitz

Mason Crest Publishers

Produced by 21st Century Publishing and Communications, Inc.

MASON CREST PUBLISHERS INC.
370 Reed Road
Broomall, Pennsylvania 19008
(866) MCP-BOOK (toll free)
www.masoncrest.com

Printed in the United States of America.

First Printing

9 8 7 6 5 4 3 2 1

Library of Congress Cataloging-in-Publication Data

Marcovitz, Hal.
   The Obama family tree / Hal Marcovitz.
      p. cm. — (Obamas, first family of hope)
   Includes bibliographical references and index.
   ISBN 978-1-4222-1481-7 (hardcover : alk. paper)
   ISBN 978-1-4222-1488-6 (pbk. : alk. paper)
   1. Obama, Barack—Family—Juvenile literature. I. Title.
E909.O22.M373 2009
973.932092—dc22
[B]   2009001461

Publisher's notes:
All quotations in this book come from original sources, and contain the spelling
and grammatical inconsistencies of the original text.

The Web sites mentioned in this book were active at the time of publication.
The publisher is not responsible for Web sites that have changed their addresses
or discontinued operation since the date of publication. The publisher will
review and update the Web site addresses each time the book is reprinted.

Contents

Introduction

On November 4, 2008, Barack Obama made history—he was the first black American to be elected president of the United States. The Obama family—Barack, wife Michelle, and daughters Malia and Sasha, became the first African-American first family.

THE FIRST FAMILY OF HOPE

The stories of the Obamas are fascinating and uniquely American. The six books in this series take you center stage and behind the scenes, with crafted and insightful storytelling, as well as hundreds of dynamic and telling photographs. Discover six unique inside perspectives on the Obama family's extraordinary journey and the Obama mania that surrounds it.

WHERE IT ALL BEGAN

Many generations ago, in the late 1600s, Barack's mother's ancestors arrived in colonial America as white emigrants from Europe, while his father's ancestors lived in villages in Kenya, Africa. Michelle's ancestors were shipped from Africa to America as slaves.

Generations later, Barack, son of a black father and a white mother, spent his childhood in Hawaii and Indonesia; while Michelle, a descendant of slaves, was growing up in Chicago. Later they both graduated from Harvard Law School, got married, and became proud parents of two beautiful daughters. Barack tackled injustice as a community organizer in Chicago, later entered politics, and was elected to the U.S. Senate.

"THE AUDACITY OF HOPE"

In 2004, at the Democratic National Convention, Barack Obama made an electrifying keynote speech, "The Audacity of Hope." He asked Americans to find unity in diversity and hope in the future. His message resonated with the attendees and millions of television viewers. Barack was catapulted from obscurity into the spotlight, and the Obama phenomenon had begun.

"YES WE CAN!"

On February 10, 2007, Barack announced his candidacy for the office of president of the United States. His family and legions of volunteers all over the country campaigned vigorously for him, and nearly two years later, the Obama family stood proudly in front of more than 240,000 supporters who gathered to hear Barack's victory speech. Tears streamed down the

The Obamas (left to right) Malia, Michelle, Sasha, and Barack, wave to their devoted fans. Barack has energized millions of people in the United States and around the world with his message of unity and hope.

faces of people who believed this was nothing short of a miracle. Tens of millions of television viewers worldwide watched and listened with a renewed sense of hope as President-elect Obama proclaimed:

> **"This victory is yours. . . . If there is anyone out there who still doubts that America is a place where all things are possible; who still wonders if the dream of our founders is alive in our time; who still questions the power of our democracy, tonight is your answer."**

OBAMA FAMILY TIMELINE

1600s to 1700s
Barack Obama's mother's ancestors immigrate to the American colonies from Europe.

1936
Barack Obama, Sr., Barack's father, is born in a small village in Kenya, Africa.

1964
Barack's parents, Barack Obama, Sr. and Ann Dunham are divorced.

1700s to 1800s
Michelle Robinson Obama's ancestors arrive in the American colonies as slaves.

1937
Michelle's mother, Marian Shields, is born.

1967
Barack's mother marries Lolo Soetoro and moves the family to Soetoro's home country, Indonesia.

1850s
Michelle's great-great grandfather is born a slave in South Carolina.

1942
Barack's mother, Ann Dunham, is born in Kansas.

1971
Barack returns to Hawaii and lives with his grandparents.

1600   **1900**   **1950**   **1982**

1912
Michelle's grandfather, Fraser Robinson Jr., is born.

1959
Barack Obama, Sr. comes to America as a student.

1979
Barack graduates from high school and enrolls in Occidental College in Los Angeles, California.

1918
Barack's grandfather, Stanley Dunham, is born.

February 21, 1961
Barack Obama, Sr. and Ann Dunham are married.

1922
Barack's grandmother, Madelyn Payne, is born.

August 4, 1961
Barack is born in Honolulu, Hawaii.

1981
Barack transfers to Columbia University in New York City.

1935
Michelle's father, Fraser Robinson III, is born.

January 17, 1964
Michelle is born in Chicago, Illinois.

1982
Barack's father dies in Kenya, Africa.

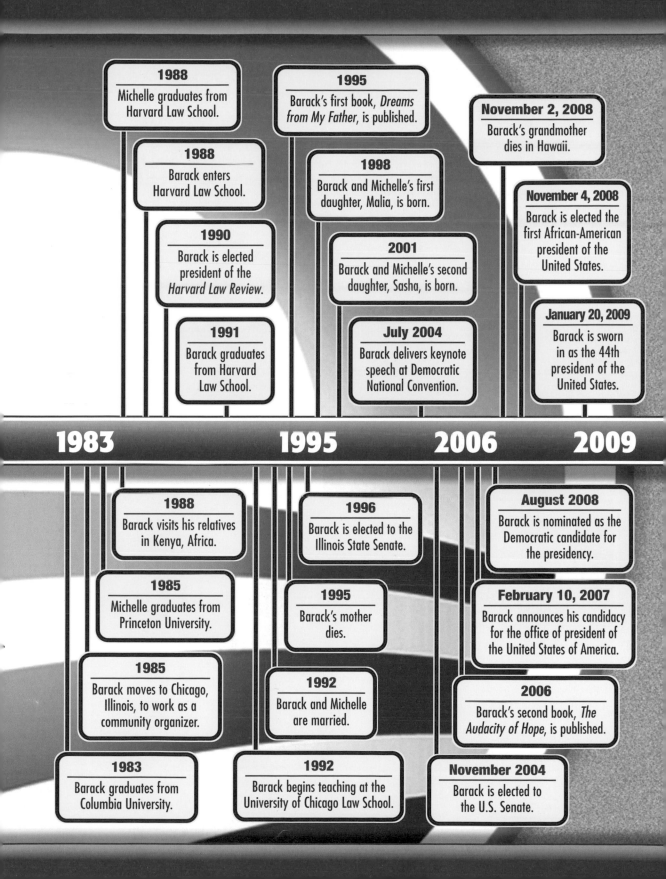

1988
Michelle graduates from Harvard Law School.

1988
Barack enters Harvard Law School.

1990
Barack is elected president of the *Harvard Law Review*.

1991
Barack graduates from Harvard Law School.

1995
Barack's first book, *Dreams from My Father*, is published.

1998
Barack and Michelle's first daughter, Malia, is born.

2001
Barack and Michelle's second daughter, Sasha, is born.

July 2004
Barack delivers keynote speech at Democratic National Convention.

November 2, 2008
Barack's grandmother dies in Hawaii.

November 4, 2008
Barack is elected the first African-American president of the United States.

January 20, 2009
Barack is sworn in as the 44th president of the United States.

1983 **1995** **2006** **2009**

1988
Barack visits his relatives in Kenya, Africa.

1985
Michelle graduates from Princeton University.

1985
Barack moves to Chicago, Illinois, to work as a community organizer.

1983
Barack graduates from Columbia University.

1996
Barack is elected to the Illinois State Senate.

1995
Barack's mother dies.

1992
Barack and Michelle are married.

1992
Barack begins teaching at the University of Chicago Law School.

August 2008
Barack is nominated as the Democratic candidate for the presidency.

February 10, 2007
Barack announces his candidacy for the office of president of the United States of America.

2006
Barack's second book, *The Audacity of Hope*, is published.

November 2004
Barack is elected to the U.S. Senate.

Kenyans celebrate Barack Obama's victory in the U.S. presidential election, November 4, 2008. Barack's father came from a small Kenyan village, and the president of Kenya said the whole country was full of pride because of Obama's Kenyan roots.

Celebration in Kenya

I n Chicago's Grant Park, 240,000 people got down to some serious partying as they celebrated the election of Barack Obama, the nation's first African-American president. Half a world away, in the tiny Kenyan village of Kogelo, the number of people dancing in the streets was far smaller, but their enthusiasm was still sky-high.

Barack's father, Barack Obama Sr., was from Kogelo. As a young man, he escaped the intense poverty of the small village to study in America, where he met and married Barack's mother. Many of Barack's relatives, including his step-grandmother, "Mama" Sarah Obama, still live in Kogelo, and the village has strong ties to the senator from Illinois who had just been elected

America's 44th president. Throughout the country, Kenyans felt immense pride that a candidate with African roots had won such an important election. Said Kenyan President Mwai Kibaki,

> **"The victory of Senator Obama is our own victory because of his roots here in Kenya. As a country, we are full of pride for his success."**

Kenya and Democracy

A former colony of Great Britain, Kenya has been independent since 1963. For much of its history, Kenya was dominated by a single political party, the Kenya African National Union (KANU), which ruled through strong-arm tactics. After an unsuccessful rebellion in 1988 a number of reforms were instituted, leading to the first truly democratic elections in 1992.

One man in the Kenyan capital of Nairobi said, "I think Kenyan people have got a lot to learn from the American election. It has shown true democracy, it does not matter how you look, it does not matter where you come from. It is about what policies you have for the people, so I think in Kenya next time we make a decision about our leaders we will know what to look for."

VICTORY SPEECH

In America, the long campaign ended the night of November 4, 2008, when the TV networks declared Barack the victor over Republican candidate Senator John McCain of Arizona. Voters had given Barack a decisive victory, endorsing his vision for change as well as his commitment to end the Iraq War, revive an ailing economy, and deliver affordable health care to Americans.

After McCain conceded, Barack and his family hurried to Grant Park where the president-elect made a victory speech before the huge crowd as well as millions of people watching on TV from home in America and elsewhere. Said Barack,

President-elect Barack Obama appears with daughters Sasha and Malia and wife Michelle at the election night rally in Grant Park, Chicago, November 4, 2008. People all over the world celebrated Barack's victory because it meant that America could again work toward peace and diplomacy.

❝ And to all those watching tonight from beyond our shores, from parliaments and palaces, to those who are huddled around radios in the forgotten corners of the world, our stories are singular, but our destiny is shared, and a new dawn of American leadership is at hand. ❞

ADVOCATING PEACE AND DIPLOMACY

Across the globe, people welcomed Barack's victory, hoping that America could re-establish its place as an advocate for peace and **diplomacy**. Under Barack's predecessor, President George W. Bush, America had launched wars in Iraq and Afghanistan. As the wars dragged on, world leaders called on Bush to seek peaceful solutions to the conflicts, but Bush resisted their pleas.

During his campaign for the presidency, Barack promised a new **foreign policy** that would engage world leaders in peace talks. In Great Britain, Prime Minister Gordon Brown said, "I know Barack Obama and we share many values and I look forward to working extremely closely with him in the coming months and years." In Germany, Chancellor Angela Merkel said,

Barack Obama waves to the crowd during his speech at the victory column in Berlin, July 24, 2008. Speaking to the crowd near where the Berlin Wall had divided the city, Obama spoke of international unity, saying that world problems can be solved only by nations working together.

" I'm convinced that through a close and trusting cooperation between the United States and Europe we will be able to confront new risks and challenges in a decisive manner and will be able to take advantage of the numerous opportunities that are opening in our world. **"**

Welcomed in Germany

Germany was the scene of one of Barack's most significant campaign events. After wrapping up the Democratic nomination, Barack toured the Middle East and Europe. On his visit to Germany, the candidate spoke before 200,000 people in the Tiergarten, a park in the German capital of Berlin. During the event, TV cameras caught the image of Germans waving American flags. In past years, foreign crowds rarely acted with friendship toward President George W. Bush, who did little to forge alliances with foreign states. Barack told the German people,

"I know my country has not perfected itself. We've made our share of mistakes, and there are times when our actions around the world have not lived up to our best intentions. But I also know how much I love America."

Back in Kenya, the people of Kogelo were far more concerned with showing the world their close affection for the new American president. As international TV news crews descended on the tiny village, the Kenyans danced and sang in Kogelo's dusty streets and planned a great feast. "People are so happy, so excited. People are in a festive mood," said Barack's uncle, Sa'id Obama. "I mean, people are going to feast literally to celebrate Barack's win."

Barack's grandparents, Madelyn and Stanley Dunham in Kansas. In his book *Dreams from My Father*, Barack wrote that both his grandparents grew up in Kansas, "less than 20 miles from each other—Madelyn in Augusta and Stanley in El Dorado, towns too small to warrant boldface on a road map."

Deep Roots in Kansas

When Samuel Hinckley and Sarah Soole married in the 1600s and settled in Massachusetts, there was no United States of America and, certainly, no thought given to how the future country would be governed. The Hinckleys would have a great impact on America's future, though, because nearly 400 years later their descendant, Barack Obama, was elected the nation's 44th president.

While it may seem impossible to trace anybody's ancestry back four centuries or more, **genealogists** have made quite a science of exploring people's roots. And so, when Barack became a serious candidate for president in 2007, genealogists started sifting through old records and were soon able to trace quite a lengthy family tree.

Barack's roots go back to the Hinckleys through his mother, Stanley Ann Dunham. Barack was born in Hawaii following his mother's marriage to Barack Obama Sr., a student from Kenya. Years earlier, Stanley Ann's family laid down roots in Kansas. The Hinckley and Dunham families joined in the mid-1700s, when Mary Smith, a great-great-granddaughter of the Hinckleys, married a New Jersey man, Jonathan Dunham. Their son, Samuel, who was Barack's great-great-great-great-great-grandfather, would go on to buy a farm in Virginia where his land was tilled by slaves.

Barack's great-great grandparents, Louisa and Jacob Dunham, 1870s. Jacob was a pharmacist in Wichita, Kansas. Two more generations of his family continued to live and work in Kansas, including Barack's grandfather, Stanley Dunham. Barack's grandmother's family, the Paynes, had also lived in Kansas for generations.

Therefore, America's first African-American president is the descendant of a slave owner. Says genealogist Christopher Child, "It shows that lots of different people can be related—people you wouldn't necessarily expect."

RIDING THE RAILS

From Virginia, the Dunhams spread out across America. They farmed in Indiana and homesteaded in Oklahoma. Barack's great-great-grandfather, Jacob Dunham, worked as a pharmacist in Wichita, Kansas. Jacob named his son Ralph Waldo Emerson Dunham. Ralph, who worked as an auto mechanic in Wichita, was named after one of America's greatest poets, Ralph Waldo Emerson. Ralph never cared for his name. "He really didn't like it that much," said his daughter, Virginia Goeldner. "It embarrassed

Kansas in the Depression

During the Great Depression of the 1930s, Kansas was part of the "Dust Bowl"—the prairie region of America hit by long droughts and dust storms, causing many farms to fail. Those where the conditions in which Stanley Dunham and Madelyn Payne spent their early years.

"The childhoods they liked to recall for my benefit portrayed small-town, Depression-era America in all its innocent glory," Barack wrote later. 'Fourth of July parades and the picture shows on the side of a barn; fireflies in a jar and the taste of vine-ripe tomatoes, sweet as apples; dust storms and hailstorms and classrooms filled with farm boys who got sewn into their woolen underwear at the beginning of winter and stank like pigs as the months wore on.'

Even the trauma of bank failures and farm foreclosures seemed romantic when spun through the loom of my grandparents' memories, a time when hardship, the great leveler that had brought people closer together, was shared by all."

him." In 1915, Ralph married Ruth Armour. Three years later, Ruth gave birth to the future president's grandfather.

Stanley Dunham was wild and reckless. Kicked out of high school for punching the principal in the nose, Stanley rode the rails hobo-style. He gambled and made **moonshine**, but in 1940 he married an 18-year-old Kansas girl, Madelyn Lee Payne. Madelyn tamed Stanley's wild side; he gave up gambling and making moonshine and found a job selling furniture.

The Paynes could trace their family back through Kansas, Illinois, and Missouri to the late 1700s. Madelyn, Barack's grandmother, claimed to be a descendant of Cherokee Indians. Years later, Barack's grandparents would tell him long and fascinating stories about their families, dazzling the boy with tales of turn-of-the-century life in Kansas. Recalled Barack,

“ An old, sepia-toned photograph on the bookshelf spoke most eloquently of their roots. It showed [Madelyn's] grandparents, of Scottish and English stock, standing in front of a ramshackle homestead, unsmiling and dressed in coarse wool, their eyes squinting in the sun-baked, flinty life that stretched before them. ”

RACISM IN TEXAS

A year after Stanley and Madelyn married, the Japanese attacked Pearl Harbor. Stanley joined the U.S. Army and served under one of the military's most distinguished leaders, General George Patton. Barack's grandfather rose to the rank of sergeant and was a member of the Allied forces that landed in France on D-Day— June 6, 1944. In the meantime, Barack's mother, Stanley Ann, was born in 1942. Recalled Barack,

“ At this point the story quickens in my mind like one of those old movies that shows a wall calendar's pages peeled back faster and faster by invisible hands, the

headlines of Hitler and Churchill and Roosevelt and Normandy spinning wildly to the drone of bombing attacks. . . . I watch as my mother is born at the army base where Gramps is stationed; my grandmother is Rosie the Riveter, working on a bomber assembly line; my grandfather sloshes around in the mud of France, part of Patton's army. **"**

Following the war, the Dunhams moved to Texas. One of Stanley Ann's playmates was a little black girl. Other children taunted Barack's mother, calling her a "nigger lover" and "dirty

Barack's grandfather, Stanley Dunham, holds his newborn daughter while his Army friends look on. During World War II, Stanley served in the army in Europe while his wife, Madelyn, helped build bombers in Kansas. When their daughter was born, Stanley had hoped for a boy, so he named her Stanley Ann.

Yankee." On one occasion, some children threw stones at Stanley Ann and her playmate. This was during the late 1940s and early 1950s—years before the **civil rights** movement. Moreover, Texas was part of the old South and, therefore, a state that practiced **segregation**. When Stanley heard that his daughter had been taunted by white children, he flew into a rage. He demanded to know which children had thrown stones at the girls. Recalled Barack,

> **Gramps was beside himself when he heard what had happened. He interrogated my mother, wrote down names. The next day he took the morning off from work to visit the school principal. He personally called the parents of some of the offending children to give them a piece of his mind. And from every adult he spoke to, he received the same response: 'You best talk to your daughter, Mr. Dunham. White girls don't play with coloreds in this town.'**

REBELLIOUS DAUGHTER

The Dunhams soon moved, finding a new home in Washington State. They settled on Mercer Island, a small community on Lake Washington near Seattle, where Stanley found a job selling furniture.

Stanley Ann spent her high school years on Mercer Island. As a teen, she rebelled against the conservative conformity of the 1950s and often fought with her parents. One point of contention was her name. Barack's grandfather had hoped for a boy, and when his daughter was born he insisted on naming her Stanley.

In 1960, soon after Stanley Ann graduated high school, the Dunhams moved to Hawaii where her father purchased a furniture store. As a young adult, Barack's mother was a member of the generation that turned the 1960s into a tumultuous decade. People who came of age in the 1960s questioned authority,

Barack's mother, Stanley Ann, poses with her parents Madelyn and Stanley Dunham. School classmates described Ann as boyish, sharp-tongued, and with a restless mind. "She was always challenging and arguing and comparing," they said. "Hers was a mind in full tilt."

supported civil rights and equality for women and minorities, and did not trust the government.

After the Dunhams arrived in Hawaii, Stanley Ann enrolled in the University of Hawaii where she met her future husband, a student from Kenya. The two fell in love and planned to marry, angering parents on both sides. During the early 1960s, mixed race marriages were still rare in American society, but the Dunhams found themselves charmed by Barack Sr.'s personal magnetism and accepted him into their family. As for Barack Sr., he faced hostility as well—his father wrote to the Dunhams, denouncing the marriage because he did not want white blood mixed into his family. Nevertheless, on February 2, 1961, Barack Sr. and Stanley Ann were married. That August, their son, Barack Hussein Obama Jr., was born.

Laws That Kept Races Apart

When Stanley Ann Dunham and Barack Obama Sr. married in 1961, marriages between black and white people were rare and in some states they were even illegal. Indeed, the so-called "anti-**miscegenation**" laws were not ruled unconstitutional until 1967, after a Virginia couple challenged their convictions under a state law that prohibited mixed-race marriages. The U.S. Supreme Court sided with the couple, Richard and Mildred Loving, and tossed out the Virginia law, also nullifying all other state statutes remaining on the books that outlawed mixed-race marriage.

Since then, many Americans of different races have felt free to marry and raise families. In 2000, the U.S. Census Bureau reported that some 7 million Americans, or about 2.4 percent of the population, designated themselves as multiracial.

Among the famous Americans who have been born into multiracial homes are baseball star Derek Jeter, reporter Soledad O'Brien, professional golfer Tiger Woods, pop singer Mariah Carey, model Tyson Beckford, actresses Halle Berry, Jennifer Beals, Rosario Dawson, Jessica Alba, and Tina and Tamara Mowry, and actors Vin Diesel and Dwayne Johnson, formerly known as the professional wrestler, The Rock.

RAISED IN AMERICA

The marriage would not last long. Barack Sr., a driven and ambitious young man, was accepted for graduate studies at Harvard University in Massachusetts; he left his young family behind in Hawaii and ultimately had little do with his wife and their young son. In 1964, Stanley Ann divorced her husband. Soon she met another foreign student, Indonesian Lolo Soetoro. In 1967, Barack's mother and Lolo married and moved to Jakarta, but by 1971 the marriage was troubled. She sent Barack and his half-sister, Maya, back to her parents' home in Hawaii so they could be raised in America and attend better schools.

After arriving in Hawaii, Barack won a **scholarship** to Punahou School, a prestigious private academy. At Punahou, Barack was regarded as an intelligent student and a good athlete. During this period, Barack grew especially close to his grandparents, particularly his grandmother, whom he called Toot. The name is a variation on the Hawaiian word for grandparent, which is "tutu." Gramps died in 1992. Sadly, Toot would not live to see Barack's political reach its peak. Toot died just two days before the November 4, 2008, election.

Barack with his grandfather, Stanley Dunham, mother Ann, and half-sister Maya Soetoro in Hawaii, early 1970s. Barack's mother sent him and Maya from Indonesia to live with their grandparents so they could get a good education. With help from his boss, Stanley arranged for Barack to go to Punahou School.

Barack poses for a family portrait during his first visit to Kenya, 1988. Barack's step-grandmother, Sarah Onyango Obama, is in the gold dress in front. During his visit, Barack learned more about his father, connected with many of his relatives, and gained pride in his African heritage.

African Heritage

Hussein Onyango Obama was a respected man in his village of Kogelo. He was a prominent farmer, an elder of his tribe, and a healer who knew how to use the herbs and plants that grew in the thick Kenyan jungle to make sick people well. At home, though, Hussein's family knew him as a much different man.

Hussein's grandson, Abongo Obama, recalled that the old man had a quick temper. He was so ornery that everyone in the family called him "the Terror." Said Abongo,

❝Wow, that guy was mean! He would make you sit at the table for dinner, and served the food on china, like an Englishman. If you said the wrong thing, or used

the wrong fork—pow! He would hit you with his stick. Sometimes when he hit you, you wouldn't even know why until the next day. **"**

MAMA SARAH

Genealogists have been able to trace Barack's family in Kenya back hundreds of years. Members of Kenya's Luo tribe, the president's ancestors, have names such as Miwiru, Kisodhi, and Obongo, but little is known about them. Once his family entered the 20th century, things started getting clearer. His grandfather, Hussein—the Terror—was born in 1895 and died in 1979. He married three times; his second wife, Akumu, provided him

Barack with his step-grandmother Sarah outside her house in Kogelo, Kenya, during his second visit to Africa in 1992. They became close; he thinks of her as his real grandmother and calls her Granny Sarah. Barack even invited her to his presidential inauguration.

with three children—two girls, and a boy named Barack Hussein Obama, who was born in 1936.

When Akumu left the family Hussein married a third time, taking for his wife Sarah Ogwel Onyango, who would raise Barack's father. Indeed, Barack regards Mama Sarah as his true grandmother and calls her "Granny." They first met when Barack visited Kenya in 1988. They forged a bond, and when Barack was inaugurated as president he invited Sarah to attend the ceremony.

Sarah was 16 years old when she married Hussein, who was old enough to be her father. It was an arranged marriage—Sarah's parents were paid by Hussein. Such marriages were common in Kenya. If Sarah had refused to marry Hussein, it is likely she would have been beaten. Recalls Sarah,

❝ Our women have carried a heavy load. If one is a fish, one does not try to fly—one swims with other fish. One only knows what one knows. Perhaps if I was young today, I would not have accepted these things. Perhaps I would only care about my feelings, and falling in love. But that's not the world I was raised in. I only know what I have seen. What I have not seen doesn't make my heart heavy. ❞

Barack's Half-Siblings

Barack Obama's father married four times and his mother married twice. So Barack has seven half-siblings who have carved out lives for themselves throughout the world. Among them are his half-sister Maya, who is a college professor in Hawaii; Mark Ndesandjo, who now runs a Web site design company in China, and George Obama, who lives in Nairobi, Kenya, where he hopes one day to become an auto mechanic.

Other half-siblings are named Abongo, Auma, Abo, and Bernard. An eighth half-sibling, David, died in a motorcycle accident before Barack visited Kenya in 1988.

VISITS TENSE AND STRAINED

In Kogelo, Mama Sarah's stepson studied hard and won a scholarship to attend the University of Hawaii. She said,

> **" Every night, and during his lunch hours, he would study his books and do the lessons in his notebooks. A few months later, he sat for the exam. . . . The exam took several months to score, and during this wait he was so nervous he could barely eat. He became so thin that we thought he would die. One day, the letter came. I was not there to see him open it. I know that when he told me the news, he was still shouting out with happiness. "**

Barack with his father, Barack Obama Sr. in 1971, during his father's month-long visit. Barack would never see his father again. Growing up fatherless, Barack struggled to define himself in multiracial, multicultural Hawaii.

Of course, Barack barely knew his father—Barack Sr. left Hawaii when Barack was a baby, and he and Stanley Ann divorced when Barack was three. When Barack was ten, his father sent word back to Hawaii that he wished to reconnect with his son. Barack Sr. spent a month in Hawaii, but never quite developed a relationship with the boy. His visits were tense and strained. During one visit, Barack sat down in front of the TV to watch *How the Grinch Stole Christmas*; Barack Sr. protested, insisting that his son go to his room to study. A family argument followed, but Barack Sr. would not give in. Barack hurried to his room, slammed the door, and wished his father would go away. After that visit, he never saw his father again.

Barack's Outspoken Father

After leaving his family in Hawaii, Barack Obama Sr. studied at Harvard University and earned a doctorate degree in economics. He returned to Kenya where he married an American woman, Ruth, and found a job with an oil company. Eventually, he became a high-ranking official in the Kenyan government, but was fired after he had a falling out with the Kenya African National Union (KANU), which controlled the regime.

His daughter Auma believes Barack Sr.'s problems grew out of a combination of his outspoken nature and heavy drinking as well as disputes among rival tribes fighting for control over the government. Auma said,

> "My dad didn't suffer fools gladly, and you have to be diplomatic. Barack is different. He is able to relate to people. I'm more like my dad. I don't have Barack's patience."

Barack Sr. returned to government service in 1978 and, despite his struggles with alcohol, seemed to have a bright future in the Kenyan government until his death in 1982.

Barack Sr. soon returned to Kenya where he suffered from alcoholism. He died in an automobile accident in 1982.

Michelle Obama gives a thumbs-up victory sign to the crowd after Barack's election night speech at Grant Park, Chicago, November 4, 2008. Michelle made history when she became first lady; she is the first descendant of a slave to live in the White House.

A Descendant of Slaves

In South Carolina, Georgetown County sits in the middle of what is known as the Low Country—its swampy marshland makes it ideal for growing rice. Before the Civil War, Georgetown County produced half of all rice consumed in America. And to grow all that rice, Georgetown County's **plantation** owners needed thousands of slaves.

One of those slaves was Jim Robinson. Born in 1850, he worked on Friendfield, one of the grandest plantations in Georgetown County. The lives of Friendfield slaves were far different from the lives of luxury enjoyed by the white owners. The slaves toiled from dawn to sunset in the swampy fields, enduring mosquitoes and snakes.

Even after the Civil War, life was still difficult. Without slaves, Friendfield collapsed. Its rice mill burned to the ground, the manor house was gutted by thieves, and a smallpox epidemic wiped out many of the plantation's families.

Somehow, Jim Robinson survived. He found work as a farmhand and by the 1880s married a woman named Louiser and was raising two sons: Gabriel, who was born in 1877, and Fraser, born in 1884. More than a century later, Jim Robinson's great-great-granddaughter, Michelle Robinson Obama, would enter the front doors of the White House as first lady.

Slaves in the White House

Michelle Robinson Obama's entry into the White House as first lady marks a significant milestone in the history of the executive mansion: she is the first descendant of a slave to be a member of the first family.

Although no descendant of a slave has lived in the White House, many slave-holding presidents have occupied the executive mansion. In fact, nine presidents, starting with George Washington, kept slaves in the White House. "House slaves" cooked and cleaned and did not have to toil in plantation fields. Still, they were considered somebody else's property and, over the years, two White House slaves rebelled against their masters and ran away.

HOUSE BOY

Gabriel and Fraser both went on to far more prosperous lives than their father knew. Gabriel became a house painter and eventually bought his own farm. Fraser also found a degree of prosperity, but he had to overcome a significant handicap: when the boy was ten years old, he broke his arm in an accident. Soon, the injury became infected and the arm was amputated.

The boy struggled with his handicap. Eventually, he was taken in by a white family, the Nesmiths, who cared for him. Fraser lived with the Nesmiths, working as their house boy. As he grew older, Fraser found a job at a lumber mill, sold newspapers, and taught himself shoemaking. Said Michelle,

A slave cabin on a dirt road once known as Slave Street on Friendfield Plantation, Georgetown, S.C., where Michelle's great-great-grandfather Jim Robinson lived as a slave. The Robinsons lived through the Civil War, segregation, and the civil rights movement, all of which eventually led to the 2008 presidential election.

❝ There are probably thousands of one-armed Frasers, all over this country, who out of slavery and emancipation, because they were smart and worked hard, those American values, were able to lift themselves up and begin to set these little foundations that led to me. ❞

Fraser married and his son, Fraser Jr.—Michelle's grandfather— was born in 1912. In Georgetown County, the Robinsons settled into a comfortable life, but the rights of African Americans were eroding in the South. Fraser Jr. had a job at a sawmill, but times were difficult and he eventually moved with his wife LaVaughn to Chicago.

DEVOTED CHILDREN

In Chicago, Fraser Jr. found work as a post office employee. In 1935, LaVaughn gave birth to Michelle's father, Fraser III. Michelle's father found a job in the city water department as a pump operator. Michelle's mother, Marian Shields, was born in Chicago's South Side in 1937. Fraser and Marian married in 1960 and raised their family in a small apartment on the South Side. Their son Craig was born in 1962; Michelle followed two years later. Craig, a college basketball coach, recalled how devoted the children were to their father. He said,

The Robinson family: Craig sits on Fraser's lap while Marian holds baby Michelle. Fraser suffered from multiple sclerosis but worked hard and attended his children's extracurricular activities; Marian was always available to help with their studies. Craig said, "Michelle has very high expectations [of her own family] based on that."

> **❝** We always felt like we couldn't let Dad down because he worked so hard for us. My sister and I, if one of us ever got in trouble with my father, we'd both be crying. We'd both be like, 'Oh, my god. Dad's upset. How could we do this to him?' **❞**

Michelle proved herself to be an intelligent young woman, excelling in school and winning a scholarship to study at Princeton University in New Jersey and later Harvard Law School in Massachusetts. She met Barack in 1989 after returning to Chicago, where she joined the staff of a law firm. They married in 1992.

KEY CONTEST

In early 2008, the South Carolina **primary** emerged as a key contest in the presidential race. By then, Fraser Jr. and LaVaughn had retired and returned to South Carolina. Although as a young girl, Michelle often visited her grandparents and listened to Fraser Jr.'s stories about the South, she has also admitted she did not know much about her family history. But during the weeks leading up to the primary, as Michelle campaigned in South Carolina, she was able to reconnect with many relatives who filled her in on her family's long history in Georgetown County. Friendfield remains a working farm and Jim Robinson's grave is located there.

A Rabbi in the Family

Michelle Obama is distantly related to Rabbi Capers Funnye, the spiritual leader of one of the few black synagogues in America, Beth Shalom B'nai Zaken Ethiopian Hebrew Congregation in Chicago.

Michelle's grandfather, Fraser Robinson Jr., is the brother of Funnye's mother, Verdelle Robinson Funnye. Capers Funnye converted to Judaism.

African Americans compose a small percentage of American Jews. Of the 5 million American Jews, it is believed that about 200,000 are African Americans.

Barack at his high school graduation in 1979. High school was a difficult time of confusion about his racial identity. He felt lost, and his grades fell. At his mother's urging Barack went to college on the mainland, where he found a new direction in political activism.

Drawn to Political Activism

When Barack stepped onto the Occidental College campus in the fall of 1979, he had just turned 18. Months before, as Barack was finishing high school in Hawaii, he had fallen into a life of parties, drinking, and occasional drug use. He had become a slacker and was even thinking about skipping college and finding a job.

By then, his mother had moved back to Hawaii, and she finally confronted him. "Your grades are slipping," she said. "You haven't even started on your college applications. . . . You can't just sit around like some good-time Charlie, waiting for luck to see you through."

Her words stung Barack. He buckled down, applied to several colleges, and finally picked Occidental, a small school in California.

Stanley Ann

After divorcing Lolo Soetoro, Barack's mother returned to Hawaii and got her master's degree in anthropology, a science that probes the origins of life. Barack and Maya lived with her for a time, but then she returned to Indonesia to pursue a doctorate degree. In Indonesia, she became a crusader for the rights of poor women. Although Barack saw her infrequently during this period, her sense of social justice left a deep impression on him.

Clearly, she was a woman whose ideas and lifestyle were well ahead of her time. Today, a single mother of biracial children pursuing an advanced college degree is part of the fabric of America; back in the 1980s, it was still something of a rarity.

In 1992, Barack's mother was finally awarded her Ph.D. Two years later, while having dinner at a friend's house, she felt a pain in her stomach. Stanley Ann learned that she was suffering from ovarian and uterine cancer. She died a year later, at the age of 52. In the final months of her life, she reconnected with her son, who by now was married and practicing law in Chicago. But Barack could not be at his mother's side when she died—a circumstance he has long regretted.

At Occidental, he got involved in political activism, particularly the campaign to convince American companies to divest themselves of business in South Africa. At this time, South Africa still maintained an **apartheid** government—its black citizens were not allowed to vote or hold public office. Caught up in the spirit of activism, Barack headed the anti-apartheid campaign on the Occidental campus. He said,

> **❝As the months passed I found myself drawn into a larger role . . . drafting letters to the faculty, printing up flyers, arguing strategy—I noticed that people had begun listening to my opinions. It was a discovery that made me hungry for words. Not words to hide behind but words that could carry a message, support an idea. ❞**

Barack's mother, Ann Dunham, late 1970s. Obama wrote about his mother, "She helped me understand that America is great not because it is perfect but because it can always be made better, and that the unfinished work of perfecting our union falls on each of us."

"LIKE A MONK"

After two years at Occidental, Barack transferred to Columbia University in New York. At Occidental, Barack had chilled mostly with African-American students and felt a need to probe further into the roots of black culture. He believed those opportunities were limited at Occidental. Before enrolling at Columbia, he preferred to be called Barry, but once he arrived in New York he went by his true name. He may have been an activist at Occidental, but he still found time for parties and basketball. At Columbia, he concentrated on his studies. He recalled,

> **66** **Mostly, my years at Columbia were an intense period of study. When I transferred, I decided to buckle down and get serious. I spent a lot of time in the library. I didn't socialize that much. I was like a monk. 99**

Barack during a visit from his grandparents Stanley and Madelyn Dunham during his Columbia years, when he studied very hard. His former roommate Phil Boerner described their "late-night philosophical discussions." "Barack listened carefully to all points of view, and he was funny, smart, thoughtful, and well-liked."

A few months before he graduated in 1983, news reached him that his father had died in Kenya. Barack had not seen his father in more than a decade. Years later, when his half-sister Auma visited him in Chicago, he learned the truth about Barack Obama Sr. He said,

> **"All my life, I had carried a single image of my father . . . the brilliant scholar, the generous friend, the upstanding leader. That image had suddenly vanished. Replaced by . . . what? A bitter drunk? An abusive husband? A defeated, lonely bureaucrat? To think that all my life I had been wrestling with nothing more than a ghost! The king is overthrown, I thought."**

COMMUNITY ORGANIZER

As he prepared to leave Columbia, Barack felt a pull toward political activism. He believed there was real power in American communities—that if people were organized, they could take control of their lives and bring about positive change. He sent applications to several nonprofit organizations but received no offers. Instead, he took a job as a writer with a company that provides financial information to corporations; he prospered there and even won a promotion.

Still, Barack felt committed to community activism, so after a year he quit his corporate job. Eventually, a friend offered him work as an organizer for the Developing Communities Project, a group helping to improve housing and employment conditions for poor people in Chicago. Finally, Barack found the type of cause he felt best suited to tackle.

He spent five years working as a community organizer and although he felt he made a positive impact on people's lives, it seemed to Barack that the way to accomplish more widespread change was to pursue change through the nation's laws. He applied to several law schools and in 1988 was accepted by Harvard University in Massachusetts. He said,

"I had things to learn in law school, things that would help me bring about real change. I would learn about interest rates, corporate mergers, the legislative process; about the way businesses and banks were put together; how real estate ventures succeeded or failed. I would learn power's currency in all its intricacy and detail, knowledge that would have compromised me before coming to Chicago but I could now bring back to where it was needed."

Maya Soetoro-Ng

Of all Barack Obama's half-siblings, he feels closest to Maya Soetoro-Ng, the daughter of his mother Stanley Ann Dunham and her second husband, Indonesian Lolo Soetoro. Barack is nine years older than Maya. Stanley Ann and Lolo divorced when Maya was nine years old. With his mother absent from the lives of both children, Barack found himself playing more of the role of father than older brother to Maya. Today, Maya is a college professor at the University of Hawaii. Her husband, Konrad Ng, is a college professor and Canadian citizen whose parents were born in Malaysia.

JOURNEY TO KENYA

Before beginning his law studies at Harvard, Barack traveled to Kenya and his father's village of Kogelo. Barack met his many half-siblings, cousins, nieces, and nephews as well as his step-grandmother Mama Sarah.

He learned about the death of a half-brother, David, and met David's mother, the American woman Ruth his father had married after divorcing Stanley Ann. As he visited Ruth, and paged through a photo album, Barack found himself growing sad—seeing pictures of family members who despite their relationships to one another, were just not quite a family. He said,

❝ They were reflections, I realized, of my own long-held fantasies, fantasies that I'd kept secret even from myself. The fantasy of [my father's] having taken my mother and me back with him to Kenya. The wish that my mother and father, sisters and brothers, were all under one roof. Here it was, I thought, what might have been. And the recognition of how wrong it had all turned out, the harsh evidence of life as it had really been lived, made me so sad that after only a few minutes I had to look away. ❞

Barack and half-sister Maya Soetoro in 1987. Maya said of her brother, "He was always pushing me to . . . exceed my own lazy inclinations . . . and find my voice and my passion." Maya participated in the 2008 Democratic National Convention and Barack's presidential campaign.

ROMANCE

After Barack's first year at Harvard he found a summer job at a Chicago law firm, where he was mentored by a young African-American attorney, Michelle Robinson. A romance soon developed.

Michelle had grown up in Chicago, resisting the lure of the streets to excel in school. Michelle found few other African-American students enrolled when she arrived at Princeton in the fall of 1981. She became an advocate for other black students, criticizing the school's administration for giving them little support on the campus. She wrote,

Michelle and Barack during the Christmas holidays in the early 1990s. When they started dating, Michelle thought Barack was just another smooth-talking guy. But later she learned he was a good communicator. And, she said, " He turned out to be an elite individual with strong moral values."

    ❝ I have found that at Princeton, no matter how liberal and open-minded some of my white professors and classmates try to be toward me, I sometimes feel like a visitor on campus, as if I really don't belong. ❞

    Still, she excelled at Princeton and, after graduation, enrolled at Harvard Law School.

    On their first date, Barack took her out for ice cream and a movie. She was at first wary of him, believing Barack to be just another smooth-talking single guy, but soon realized the depth of his intellect and his interest in most any subject. She said,

    ❝ I call him 'The Fact Guy.' He seems to have a fact about everything. He can argue and debate about anything. It doesn't matter if he agrees with you, he can still argue with you. Sometimes, he's even right. ❞

Law Review President

Returning to Harvard after his summer job, Barack was elected president of the *Harvard Law Review* by his fellow students. The *Law Review* is the college's prestigious publication that provides commentary on important legal cases; during its more than a century of existence, an African American had never been elected president. The competition among the *Law Review*'s 70 staff members was fierce, but Barack found widespread support from fellow students who were drawn to him because of his intelligence and leadership abilities. Barack hoped his election would help open new doors for African Americans at Harvard.

    After graduation, Barack returned to Chicago and married Michelle. He headed a voter registration drive before taking a job with a law firm specializing in civil rights cases. And he would soon answer a call that would lead him into elective politics and a role that would make it possible for him to truly champion change in people's lives.

Barack holds daughter Malia, while Michelle holds Sasha in 2002. Barack always wanted to give his daughters the stable childhood he never had, with two loving parents, friends, and a good neighborhood. The family found a comfortable life on Chicago's South Side.

A New Generation

As a community organizer, Barack helped people improve their housing and employment opportunities. As a lawyer, he worked to protect his clients' civil rights. Barack believed he could do the most good by serving as a **legislator**, crafting laws that would give all people an equal chance of achieving good jobs, homes, and educations.

In 1996, the seat representing the South Side of Chicago opened up in the state Senate. Barack's work in the voter registration drive had raised his profile among Democratic leaders. When Alice Palmer, the state senator for the South Side, chose not to seek re-election, Barack found support among Illinois Democratic leaders. He entered the race and easily won the post.

As Barack and Michelle settled into their lives on the South Side, he was determined to raise the type of family he had never known as a boy. He had spent his boyhood living in Indonesia with a stepfather and then in Hawaii in the home of his grandparents, dealing with an absentee father and at times an absentee mother. He did not want that for his family—he wanted children, and he wanted them to grow up in a two-parent household in an established neighborhood, with friends, birthday parties, and a backyard.

On July 4, 1998, Michelle gave birth to the Obamas' first child, daughter Malia. Recalled Barack,

> **❝ Malia was born, a Fourth of July baby, so calm and so beautiful, with big, hypnotic eyes that seemed to read the world the moment they opened. ❞**

TIMES OF TENSION

Barack's future seemed bright but there were times of tension. Michelle found herself raising Malia on her own as Barack spent much of his time in the state capital of Springfield, some 150 miles from the family's Chicago home. Michelle demanded that Barack start paying more attention to his family. Barack agreed, but renewing his commitment to his family cost him politically.

In 1999, he took his family to Hawaii for a vacation at a time when a crucial bill on gun control legislation came to the Senate floor for a vote. When Malia, then 18 months old, became ill, Barack refused to cut his vacation short so that he could return to Springfield for the vote. A year later, he entered his first race for Congress, a Democratic primary against U.S. Representative Bobby Rush, and lost after Rush was able to use his absence on the gun control vote against him. Said Barack,

> **❝ There are times when I want to do everything and be everything. I want to have time to read and swim with the kids and not disappoint my voters and do a really careful job on each and every thing that I do. And that can sometimes get me into trouble. ❞**

Malia Obama with her mom, Michelle. After tension arose about Barack spending so much time away from home on political business, he rededicated himself to the family. Later he often gave speeches that emphasized the important role of parents—especially fathers— in their children's lives.

A year after the unsuccessful campaign against Rush, Michelle delivered the Obama family's second daughter, Sasha.

A BUSY FAMILY

During the first few years of the 2000 decade, Malia's and Sasha's father was one of the busiest politicians in America. Between Malia's birth in 1999 and the launch of his presidential campaign in early 2007, Barack ran in four political campaigns—twice more for the state Senate, once for Rush's seat, and once for the U.S. Senate in 2004.

Moreover, Michelle Obama led a busy professional life as well—after graduating from Harvard in 1988 she worked as an attorney for three years, then joined the staff of Chicago Mayor

Richard M. Daley as an aide. After two years on Daley's staff, Michelle headed a nonprofit jobs training program, then spent many years at the University of Chicago, first as an associate dean and then a hospital administrator.

A CLOSE-KNIT FAMILY

Michelle had grown up in a close-knit family in which her parents had always found time for the children. Barack and Michelle were determined to forge a similar home life for their children. Although Barack had made a commitment to spend more time with his children—he personally planned Sasha's fifth birthday party—there is no question that Michelle has made the most sacrifices for the sake of the family. Said Barack,

> **" It was Michelle and not I who was expected to make the necessary adjustments. Sure, I helped, but it was always on my terms, on my schedule. Meanwhile, she was the one who had to put her career on hold. She was the one who had to make sure that the kids were fed and bathed every night. "**

PROSPERITY

Barack and Michelle had both grown up in modest circumstances. As adults, the two Harvard-educated lawyers prospered. Before resigning from the University of Chicago to work full time in Barack's presidential campaign, Michelle had been earning a salary of nearly $300,000 a year. Moreover, Barack had authored two books that turned out to be bestsellers, earning millions of dollars for the family and enabling the Obamas to buy a $1.6 million home in the Hyde Park section of Chicago.

The Obamas' prosperity also meant that the two girls could attend private school in Chicago. They have both taken piano and tennis lessons. Malia also plays soccer and has studied dance and drama, while Sasha has taken gymnastics and tap dancing. Over the summer, the girls attended day camps.

The Obamas on the cover of *People* magazine. Barack and Michelle are devoted to their daughters. In a letter to them, Barack wrote, "I realized that my own life wouldn't count for much unless I was able to ensure that you had every opportunity for happiness and fulfillment in yours."

After moving into the White House, the girls were enrolled in Sidwell Friends School in Washington, D.C., an exclusive, and expensive, private school. The girls have known only privilege in their young lives, a stark contrast to the childhoods of their parents.

Malia and Sasha

Malia and Sasha may be sisters, but their personalities are very different. Malia is more reserved, more committed to studying, and is thinking about a career as an actress. Sasha is more outgoing. At the Democratic National Convention, she stole the show when she took the stage with mother and sister and, in a satellite hookup, playfully teased her father for forgetting which city he was in.

In 2004, Barack recalled how each of his daughters reacted when he was sworn in as a U.S. senator:

"In the Old Senate Chamber, I joined my wife, Michelle, and our two daughters for a reenactment of the ceremony and picture-taking with Vice President Cheney. True to form, then six-year-old Malia demurely shook the vice president's hand, while then three-year-old Sasha decided instead to slap palms with the man before twirling around to wave for the cameras."

A METEORIC RISE

Barack's rise through the political world has been swift. After losing the 2000 primary to Rush, he returned to the state Senate, then entered a U.S. Senate race in 2004. It was during that Senate race that he first started advocating a message of change and unity to Americans. He also made clear his opposition to the war in Iraq, a position that was far less popular in 2004 than it was in 2008. He won a hard-fought primary; then, while preparing for the fall campaign, he was invited by presidential candidate John Kerry to deliver the **keynote address** at that summer's Democratic National Convention. His dramatic speech, in which he called for Americans to unite to solve the country's enormous problems, established Barack as a national political figure.

In 2007, when he kicked off his run for the presidency, his campaign drew enormous support from young people as well as many others who felt the old-style divisive politics of the past had simply not worked. In 2008, Barack emerged from a crowded field of Democratic candidates to win his party's nomination. That fall, he defeated Republican John McCain by scoring 53 percent of the vote—the first Democrat to win the presidency with more than 50 percent of the popular vote since President Lyndon Baines Johnson won in a landslide in 1964.

Sasha and Malia ready for their first day at Sidwell Friends School, January 5, 2009. Barack explained his views on education: "I want all our children to go to schools worthy of their potential—schools that challenge them, inspire them, and instill in them a sense of wonder about the world around them."

DIVERSE AMERICAN SOCIETY

Less than three weeks after the historic 2008 election, Malia and Sasha stood behind a table at a Chicago food bank, helping their parents hand out food to poor families. Barack and Michelle insisted that the girls help out at a food bank, where they could learn values, respect for others, and the importance of helping those less fortunate than themselves.

As he campaigned for the presidency in 2008, Barack had to overcome a racial barrier that had prevented an African American

Barack Obama takes the presidential oath of office as his family looks on, January 20, 2009. The Obamas' story represents a family tree stretching from Kansas to Kogelo, a small Kenyan village, and from South Carolina slaves in the deep South, across the generations to the presidency.

from winning the White House since the nation's founding more than 200 years ago. Clearly, he appealed to a broad spectrum of people. American government has changed a lot in the past few decades—it is no longer dominated by white men. In early 2009, just weeks before Barack took the oath of office, the new Congress was sworn in. It includes 95 women—the most in history—as well as more than 40 African Americans, more than 30 Hispanics, and 11 Asian Americans.

THE INAUGURATION

On January 20, 2009, Barack Hussein Obama was officially sworn in as the 44th president of the United States of America. On the grand platform overlooking more than a million people from all walks of life who had come to Washington, D.C. to bear witness to this moment in history, Barack, Michelle, Malia, and Sasha were surrounded by their own diverse extended family.

The families that produced the nation's first family are black and white and Asian, Christian, Muslim, and Jewish. They speak English, Indonesian, French, Cantonese, German, Hebrew, and a few African languages including Swahili, Luo, and Igbo. Very few are wealthy, and some are very poor. They have come from African villages, Indonesian poverty, and poor Kansas farms; through slavery, emancipation, segregation, and the civil rights movement.

Yet the stories of this family are stories of self-determination, regardless of background, race, religion, parentage, or place of birth—a self-determination that has led them all the way to the White House and the highest office in the most powerful country in the world.

Mid-1600s Samuel Hinckley and Sarah Soole marry in Barnstable, Massachusetts; they are the first known ancestors of Barack Obama.

Mid-1700s The Hinckley and Dunham families merge with the marriage of Mary Smith, a descendant of the Hinckleys, and Jonathan Dunham, a direct ancestor of Barack's mother, Stanley Ann Dunham.

1850 Jim Robinson is born a slave in Georgetown County, South Carolina; he is the first known ancestor in America of Michelle Robinson Obama.

1895 Barack's paternal grandfather, Hussein Onyango Obama, is born in Kenya, Africa.

1918 Stanley Dunham, Barack's grandfather, is born.

1922 Madelyn Payne, Barack's grandmother, is born.

1936 Barack Hussein Obama Sr. is born in Kenya, Africa.

1942 Barack's mother, Stanley Ann Dunham, is born in Kansas.

1961 Barack Hussein Obama Sr. and Stanley Ann Dunham marry; Barack Hussein Obama Jr. is born on August 4 in Honolulu, Hawaii.

1964 Barack's parents divorce; Michelle Robinson is born in Chicago, Illinois.

1967 Barack's mother marries Lolo Soetoro and moves the family to Indonesia.

1979 Barack graduates from Punahou School in Hawaii and enrolls in Occidental College in California; later he transfers to Columbia University in New York.

1982 Barack's father dies in Kenya.

1983 Barack graduates from Columbia and takes a job in New York City.

1984 Barack resigns from his corporate job and becomes a community organizer in Chicago.

1988 Barack visits Kenya; enrolls at Harvard Law School.

1989 Barack starts dating Michelle Robinson.

1992 Barack and Michelle marry.

1995 Barack's mother dies.

1996 Barack wins his first political race, a seat in the Illinois State Senate.

1998 Older daughter Malia is born.

2001 Younger daughter Sasha is born.

2004 Barack elected to the U.S. Senate representing Illinois.

2008 Barack elected 44th president of the United States; Barack's grandmother dies two days prior to the election.

2009 On January 20, Barack is sworn in as the 44th president of the United States; the Obamas move into the White House.

- Michelle's mother, Marian Robinson, moved into the White House with the Obama family in January 2009; she is not the first president's mother-in-law to live in the executive mansion. Others have included the mothers of first ladies Bess Truman and Mamie Eisenhower.

- Barack's great-grandfather, Ralph Waldo Emerson Dunham, was a Kansas auto mechanic. Among his other ancestors named after historical figures are George Washington Overall, a Kentucky farmer, and Christopher Columbus Clark, a veteran of the Civil War.

- Barack is a distant relative of several other presidents, including George H.W. Bush, George W. Bush, Gerald Ford, James Madison, Lyndon Baines Johnson, and Harry Truman. Also, he is a distant cousin of the former vice president Richard Cheney.

- Two of Barack's distant relatives are Samuel Clemens, better known as the author Mark Twain, and cattleman Charles Goodnight, said to be the inspiration for the fictional character Woodrow Call in the Pulitzer Prize–winning novel *Lonesome Dove*. Actor Brad Pitt is also a distant cousin.

- Nine presidents kept slaves in the White House. Slaves helped build the White House as well as the U.S. Capitol. In 2005, Congress established a commission to find a way to honor the slaves who built the White House and Capitol, probably through the erection of a monument.

- Barack gave his first speech on the campus of Occidental College in Los Angeles, California. In the speech, he denounced the South African apartheid government. To dramatize the plight of black South Africans, he arranged for two white students dressed in military uniforms to drag him off the stage in midsentence.

- After transferring to Columbia University from Occidental College, Barack arranged to stay with a friend, but when he arrived in New York no one was home and he was locked out. With no money for a hotel, he spent his first night in New York curled up in an alley.

- Before Barack's election as president of the *Harvard Law Review*, an African American had never been selected to head the publication. But in the election for *Law Review* president, the two finalists were Barack and another African-American student, Kenneth Mack.

apartheid—In South Africa, the official policy of the government that denied equality to black citizens, barring them from voting, holding public office, and enjoying most other benefits reserved for whites. Under international pressure, South Africa ended apartheid rule in 1994.

civil rights—Rights defined by the U.S. Constitution that guarantee all Americans equal treatment under law, such as the right to vote and the rights of women to earn pay equal to the salaries earned by men.

diplomacy—Method used by countries to resolve their differences peacefully without resorting to armed conflict.

foreign policy—The official position taken by one country in its relationships with other countries.

genealogists—Professionals who explore the family backgrounds of individuals; working with birth records and similar sources, genealogists are often able to trace family histories over hundreds of years.

keynote address—The major speech delivered at the opening of the national political conventions, or similar events, intended to set the tone for the conventions and inspire the delegates and others who attend.

legislator—Member of a representative body of government, such as Congress or a state assembly, who participates in the drafting of new laws.

miscegenation—a mixture of races.

moonshine—Liquor made illegally, usually in secret.

plantation—Large farm found in the South; prior to the Civil War, plantations were maintained mostly by slave labor.

primary—Process used by many states to select nominees for fall elections and award delegates to presidential candidates.

scholarship—Financial assistance offered by a school or college to help a student pay the cost of tuition.

segregation—Official policy followed by many states that prohibited African Americans from attending the same schools as whites and from sharing other common services of society, such as buses, restaurants, and theaters. Segregation was outlawed under a series of court decisions in the 1950s and 1960s as well as by laws adopted by Congress in the 1960s.

Books and Periodicals

Murray, Shailagh. "A Family Tree Rooted in American Soil: Michelle Obama Learns About Her Slave Ancestors, Herself and Her Country," *Washington Post* (October 2, 2008): p. C-1.

Obama, Barack. *The Audacity of Hope: Thoughts on Reclaiming the American Dream*. New York: Three Rivers Press, 2006.

———. *Dreams from My Father: A Story of Race and Inheritance*. New York: Crown, 2004.

Oppong, Joseph R. and Esther D. *Kenya*. New York: Chelsea House, 2003.

Richmond, Robert W. *Kansas: A Land of Contrasts*. Wheeling, Ill.: Harlan Davidson, 1999.

Ripley, Amanda. "The Family Obama," *Time* (September 1, 2008): p. 46.

Ripley, Amanda, and Zamira Loebis and Jason Tedjasukmana. "A Mother's Story," *Time* (April 21, 2008): p. 36.

Sullivan, Robert, editor. *The American Journey of Barack Obama: From Boyhood to the White House*. New York: Little, Brown and Company, 2008.

Web Sites

www.barackobama.com

Obama for America. The campaign committee that worked to elect Barack Obama to the presidency maintains a Web site that explains the issues the 44th president must tackle during his administration.

www.state.gov/r/pa/ei/bgn/2962.htm

The U.S. State Department provides many resources on Kenya on this Web site, including data on the geography and population of the African nation. Students can find a history of Kenya, including information on the country's troubled political history.

www.suntimes.com/images/cds/special/family_tree.html

The *Chicago Sun-Times* maintains this Web site, tracing Barack's family tree back many generations on both his mother's and father's sides.

www.chicagotribune.com/news/politics/obama

The Obamas. The *Chicago Tribune* has made its extensive archive of stories about Barack and the members of his family available on this Web site.

www.whitehouse.gov

Official Web site of the White House chronicles the activities of the first family and provides information on many key issues that are addressed by the president.

page

2: Obama for America/PRMS	**32:** Oliver Douliery/Abaca Press/MCT
7: Bill Greenblatt/UPI Photo	**35:** Chicago Tribune/MCT
10: EFE/STR	**36:** Obama for America/PRMS
13: Olivier Douliery/Abaca Press/MCT	**38:** Obama for America/PRMS
14: Alex Korting/ASP	**41:** Obama for America/PRMS
16: Obama for America/PRMS	**42:** Obama for America/PRMS
18: Obama for America/PRMS	**45:** Obama for America/PRMS
21: Obama for America/PRMS	**46:** Obama for America/PRMS
23: Obama for America/PRMS	**48:** Obama for America/PRMS
25: Obama for America/PRMS	**51:** Obama for America/PRMS
26: Obama for America/PRMS	**53:** People Magazine/NMI
28: Obama for America/PRMS	**55:** Callie Shell/Obama Transition Office/NMI
30: Obama for America/PRMS	**56:** Chuck Kennedy/MCT

Front cover: Obama for America/PRMS

ABOUT THE AUTHOR

Hal Marcovitz is a former newspaper reporter who has written more than 100 books for young readers. In 2005, *Nancy Pelosi*, his biography of House Speaker Nancy Pelosi, was named to *Booklist* magazine's list of recommended feminist books for young readers. He lives in Chalfont, Pennsylvania, with his wife Gail and daughter Ashley.